# EVERYDAY EASY MEALS

For more delicious recipes and easy meal ideas, visit the
*Campbell's* Web site at **www.campbellsoup.com**

# *Campbell's*®

# Homemade in 20 Minutes

## CHICKEN & BROCCOLI ALFREDO

**Prep/Cook Time:** 20 minutes    *20 minutes or less!*

½ package *uncooked* linguine (8 ounces)
1 cup fresh *or* frozen broccoli flowerets
2 tablespoons butter *or* margarine
1 pound skinless, boneless chicken breasts, cubed
1 can (10¾ ounces) CAMPBELL'S Condensed Cream of Mushroom Soup *or* 98% Fat Free Cream of Mushroom Soup
½ cup milk
½ cup grated Parmesan cheese
¼ teaspoon freshly ground pepper

1. Prepare linguine according to package directions. Add broccoli for last 4 minutes of cooking time.

2. In medium skillet over medium-high heat, heat butter. Add chicken and cook until browned, stirring often. Drain.

3. Add soup, milk, cheese, pepper and linguine mixture and cook through, stirring occasionally. Serve with additional Parmesan cheese.

*Serves 4*

**Chicken & Broccoli Alfredo**

1 tablespoon vegetable oil
4 skinless, boneless chicken breast halves (about 1 pound)
1 can (10¾ ounces) CAMPBELL'S Condensed Cream of Chicken Soup *or* 98% Fat Free Cream of Chicken Soup
1½ cups water*
¼ teaspoon paprika
¼ teaspoon pepper
1½ cups *uncooked* Minute® Original Rice
2 cups fresh *or* thawed frozen broccoli flowerets

1. In medium skillet over medium-high heat, heat oil. Add chicken and cook 8 minutes or until browned. Set chicken aside. Pour off fat.

2. Add soup, water, paprika and pepper. Heat to a boil.

3. Stir in rice and broccoli. Place chicken on rice mixture. Season chicken with additional paprika and pepper. Reduce heat to low. Cover and cook 5 minutes or until chicken is no longer pink.
*Serves 4*

*For creamier rice, increase water to 1⅔ cups.

**15-Minute Chicken & Rice Dinner**

# 15-MINUTE HERBED CHICKEN

**Prep/Cook Time:** 15 minutes      *20 minutes or less!*

>    1 tablespoon vegetable oil
>    4 skinless, boneless chicken breast halves (about
>        1 pound)
>    1 can (10¾ ounces) CAMPBELL'S Condensed Cream of
>        Chicken with Herbs Soup
>    ½ cup milk
>    Broth Simmered Rice*

**1** In medium skillet over medium-high heat, heat oil. Add chicken and cook 8 minutes or until browned. Set chicken aside. Pour off fat.

**2** Add soup and milk. Heat to a boil. Return chicken to pan. Reduce heat to low. Cover and cook 5 minutes or until chicken is no longer pink.                                              *Serves 4*

**\*Broth Simmered Rice:** In medium saucepan over medium-high heat, heat 1 can CAMPBELL'S Condensed Chicken Broth and 1 cup water to a boil. Stir in 2 cups *uncooked* Minute® Original Rice. Cover and remove from heat. Let stand 5 minutes. Fluff with fork.

**Creamy Mushroom-Garlic Chicken:** Substitute 1 can (10¾ ounces) CAMPBELL'S Condensed Cream of Mushroom with Roasted Garlic Soup for Cream of Chicken with Herbs Soup.

**Quick Herbed Chicken Dijon:** In step 2 add 1 tablespoon Dijon-style mustard with the soup and milk.

**Top to bottom: Hearty Chicken Noodle Soup (page 11),
Broth Simmered Rice and 15-Minute Herbed Chicken**

# SPEEDY CHICKEN ENCHILADAS

**Prep/Cook Time:** 20 minutes   *20 minutes or less!*

**1 pound skinless, boneless chicken breasts, cubed**
**1 can (10¾ ounces) CAMPBELL'S Condensed Cream of Chicken Soup *or* 98% Fat Free Cream of Chicken Soup**
**1 cup PACE Thick & Chunky Salsa *or* Picante Sauce**
**8 flour tortillas (6-inch)**
**1 can (10¾ ounces) CAMPBELL'S Condensed Cheddar Cheese Soup**

**1** In medium nonstick skillet over medium-high heat, cook chicken until browned and juices evaporate, stirring often. Add chicken soup and ½ *cup* salsa. Heat to a boil, stirring occasionally.

**2** Along one side of each tortilla, spread about ⅓ *cup* chicken mixture. Roll up each tortilla around filling and place seam-side down in 2-quart microwave-safe baking dish.

**3** Mix cheese soup and remaining salsa and pour over enchiladas.

**4** Cover and microwave on HIGH 5 minutes or until hot.

*Serves 4*

*Warm tortillas for easier handling. Stack tortillas and wrap in damp, microwave-safe paper towels. Microwave on HIGH for 15 seconds for 2 tortillas; add 15 seconds to time for every 2 additional tortillas.*

**Top to bottom: Speedy Chicken Enchiladas and Beef & Cheddar Soft Tacos (page 10)**

## BEEF & CHEDDAR SOFT TACOS

*(photo on page 9)*

**Prep/Cook Time:** 15 minutes      *20 minutes or less!*

> 1 pound ground beef
> 1 can (10¾ ounces) CAMPBELL'S Condensed Cheddar
>     Cheese Soup
> ½ cup PACE Thick & Chunky Salsa *or* Picante Sauce
> 8 flour tortillas (8-inch)
> 2 cups shredded lettuce (about ½ small head)

**1** In medium skillet over medium-high heat, cook beef until browned, stirring to separate meat. Pour off fat.

**2** Add soup and salsa. Reduce heat to low and heat through.

**3** Spoon **about ⅓ cup** meat mixture down center of each tortilla. Top with lettuce. Fold tortilla around filling. Serve with additional salsa.                              *Serves 4*

## SAUCY PORK CHOPS

*(photo on page 13)*

**Prep/Cook Time:** 15 minutes      *20 minutes or less!*

> 1 tablespoon vegetable oil
> 4 pork chops, ½ inch thick (about 1 pound)
> 1 can (10¾ ounces) CAMPBELL'S Condensed Cream of
>     Onion Soup
> ¼ cup water

**1** In medium skillet over medium-high heat, heat oil. Add chops and cook 8 minutes or until browned. Set chops aside. Pour off fat.

**2** Add soup and water. Heat to a boil. Return chops to pan. Reduce heat to low. Cover and cook 5 minutes or until chops are no longer pink.                              *Serves 4*

# HEARTY CHICKEN NOODLE SOUP

*(photo on page 7)*

**Prep/Cook Time:** 20 minutes     *20 minutes or less!*

**2 cans (10½ ounces *each*) CAMPBELL'S Condensed
    Chicken Broth**
**1 cup water**
    **Generous dash pepper**
**1 medium carrot, sliced (about ½ cup)**
**1 stalk celery, sliced (about ½ cup)**
**2 skinless, boneless chicken breast halves, cut up**
**½ cup *uncooked* medium egg noodles**

**1** In medium saucepan mix broth, water, pepper, carrot, celery and chicken. Over medium-high heat, heat to a boil.

**2** Stir in noodles. Reduce heat to medium. Cook 10 minutes or until noodles are done, stirring often.          *Serves 4*

*Save time by using precut carrots and celery from your supermarket salad bar.*

# SEAFOOD TOMATO ALFREDO

**Prep/Cook Time:** 20 minutes    *20 minutes or less!*

1 tablespoon margarine *or* butter
1 medium onion, chopped (about ½ cup)
1 can (10¾ ounces) **CAMPBELL'S Condensed Cream of Mushroom with Roasted Garlic Soup**
½ cup milk
1 cup diced canned tomatoes
1 pound firm white fish (cod, haddock *or* halibut), cut into 2-inch pieces
4 cups hot cooked linguine (about 8 ounces uncooked)

**1** In medium skillet over medium-high heat, heat margarine. Add onion and cook until tender.

**2** Add soup, milk and tomatoes. Heat to a boil. Add fish. Reduce heat to low. Cook 10 minutes or until fish flakes easily when tested with a fork. Serve over linguine.        *Serves 4*

*Salted water takes longer to boil. To save time, don't salt water until after it is boiling.*

**Top to bottom: Saucy Pork Chop (page 10) and Seafood Tomato Alfredo**

# ASPARAGUS & HAM POTATO TOPPER

**Prep/Cook Time:** 10 minutes     *20 minutes or less!*

> 4 hot baked potatoes, split
> 1 cup diced cooked ham
> 1 can (10¾ ounces) CAMPBELL'S Condensed Cream of
>     Asparagus Soup
> **Shredded Cheddar *or* Swiss cheese (optional)**

1 Place hot baked potatoes on microwave-safe plate. Carefully fluff up potatoes with fork.

2 Top each potato with ham. Stir soup in can until smooth. Spoon soup over potatoes. Top with cheese, if desired. Microwave on HIGH 4 minutes or until hot.          *Serves 4*

# LEMON ASPARAGUS CHICKEN

**Prep/Cook Time:** 20 minutes     *20 minutes or less!*

> 1 tablespoon vegetable oil
> 4 skinless, boneless chicken breast halves (about
>     1 pound)
> 1 can (10¾ ounces) CAMPBELL'S Condensed Cream of
>     Asparagus Soup
> ¼ cup milk
> 1 tablespoon lemon juice
> ⅛ teaspoon pepper

1 In medium skillet over medium-high heat, heat oil. Add chicken and cook 8 minutes or until browned. Set chicken aside. Pour off fat.

2 Add soup, milk, lemon juice and pepper. Heat to a boil. Return chicken to pan. Reduce heat to low. Cover and cook 5 minutes or until chicken is no longer pink.          *Serves 4*

**Top to bottom: Asparagus & Ham Potato Topper and
Lemon Asparagus Chicken**

# EASY SKILLET BEEF & HASH BROWNS

*20 minutes or less!*

1 pound ground beef
1 can (10¾ ounces) CAMPBELL'S Condensed Cream of
    Celery Soup *or* 98% Fat Free Cream of Celery Soup
½ cup water
¼ cup ketchup
1 tablespoon Worcestershire sauce
2 cups frozen diced potatoes (hash browns)
3 slices process American cheese (about 3 ounces)

**1** In medium skillet over medium-high heat, cook beef until browned, stirring to separate meat. Pour off fat.

**2** Add soup, water, ketchup and Worcestershire. Heat to a boil. Stir in potatoes. Reduce heat to medium-low. Cover and cook 10 minutes or until potatoes are done, stirring occasionally. Top with cheese. *Serves 4*

Top to bottom: Quick Beef Skillet (page 18) and
Easy Skillet Beef & Hash Browns

# QUICK BEEF SKILLET

*(photo on page 17)*

**Prep/Cook Time:** 15 minutes       *20 minutes or less!*

- **1 pound ground beef**
- **1 can (10¾ ounces) CAMPBELL'S Condensed Tomato Soup**
- **¼ cup water**
- **1 tablespoon Worcestershire sauce**
- **¼ teaspoon pepper**
- **1 can (about 15 ounces) sliced potatoes, drained**
- **1 can (about 8 ounces) sliced carrots, drained**

**1** In medium skillet over medium-high heat, cook beef until browned, stirring to separate meat. Pour off fat.

**2** Add soup, water, Worcestershire, pepper, potatoes and carrots. Reduce heat to low and heat through.       *Serves 4*

*Store ground meat in the coldest part of the refrigerator (35°F.) for no longer than 2 days.*

# ITALIAN BURGER MELT

(photo on page 21)

**Prep/Cook Time:** 20 minutes    *20 minutes or less!*

    **1 pound ground beef**
    **1 can (11⅛ ounces) CAMPBELL'S Condensed Italian Tomato Soup**
  **¼ cup water**
    **4 slices mozzarella, process American *or* Monterey Jack cheese (about 4 ounces)**
    **4 hamburger rolls, split and toasted**

**1** Shape beef into 4 patties, ½ inch thick.

**2** In medium skillet over medium-high heat, cook patties until browned. Set patties aside. Pour off fat.

**3** Add soup and water. Heat to a boil. Return patties to pan. Reduce heat to low. Cover and cook 10 minutes or until patties are no longer pink (160°F.).

**4** Place cheese on patties and cook until cheese is melted. Place patties on 4 roll halves. Top with soup mixture and remaining roll halves.

*Makes 4 sandwiches*

**Serving Idea:** Serve with **Swanson Simple Seasoned Pasta.** In medium saucepan over medium-high heat, heat to a boil 2 cans (14½ ounces *each*) SWANSON Seasoned Chicken Broth with Italian Herbs. Stir in 3 cups *uncooked* corkscrew pasta. Reduce heat to medium. Simmer gently 10 minutes or until pasta is done, stirring occasionally. Serves about 6.

# FRENCH ONION BURGERS

**Prep/Cook Time:** 20 minutes    *20 minutes or less!*

**1 pound ground beef**
**1 can (10½ ounces) CAMPBELL'S Condensed French
   Onion Soup**
**4 round hard rolls, split**
**4 slices cheese (use your favorite)**

1 Shape beef into 4 patties, ½ inch thick.

2 In medium skillet over medium-high heat, cook patties until browned. Set patties aside. Pour off fat.

3 Add soup. Heat to a boil. Return patties to pan. Reduce heat to low. Cover and cook 10 minutes or until patties are no longer pink (160°F.).

4 Place cheese on patties and cook until cheese is melted. Place patties on 4 roll halves. Serve with soup mixture for dipping.
*Makes 4 sandwiches*

**Top to bottom: Italian Burger Melt (page 19) and
French Onion Burger**

# *Campbell's*®

# Speedy Skillets

## COUNTRY SKILLET SUPPER

**Prep Time:** 5 minutes     **Cook Time:** 25 minutes

- 1 **pound ground beef**
- 1 **medium onion, chopped (about ½ cup)**
- ⅛ **teaspoon garlic powder** *or* **1 clove garlic, minced**
- 1 **can (10¾ ounces) CAMPBELL'S Condensed Golden Mushroom Soup**
- 1 **can (10½ ounces) CAMPBELL'S Condensed Beef Broth**
- 1 **can (14½ ounces) diced tomatoes**
- 1 **small zucchini, sliced (about 1 cup)**
- ½ **teaspoon dried thyme leaves, crushed**
- 1½ **cups *uncooked* corkscrew pasta**

**1** In medium skillet over medium-high heat, cook beef, onion and garlic powder until beef is browned, stirring to separate meat. Pour off fat.

**2** Add soup, broth, tomatoes, zucchini and thyme. Heat to a boil. Stir in pasta. Reduce heat to low. Cook 15 minutes or until pasta is done, stirring often.                                    *Serves 4*

**Country Skillet Supper Provençal:** Top with sliced pitted ripe olives.

**Country Skillet Supper**

# JAMBALAYA ONE DISH

**Prep Time:** 10 minutes    **Cook Time:** 20 minutes

- 1 tablespoon vegetable oil
- ½ pound skinless, boneless chicken breasts, cut up
- ½ pound hot Italian pork sausage, sliced
- ¼ teaspoon garlic powder *or* 2 cloves garlic, minced
- 1 can (10½ ounces) CAMPBELL'S Condensed French Onion Soup
- ⅓ cup PACE Picante Sauce *or* Thick & Chunky Salsa
- 1 cup *uncooked* Minute® Original Rice
- ½ cup frozen peas
- ½ pound frozen cooked large shrimp

**1** In medium skillet over medium-high heat, heat oil. Add chicken, sausage and garlic powder and cook 5 minutes or until browned, stirring often. Pour off fat.

**2** Add soup and picante sauce. Heat to a boil. Stir in rice, peas and shrimp. Reduce heat to low. Cover and cook 5 minutes or until chicken and sausage are no longer pink and most of liquid is absorbed.                                      *Serves 4*

**Jambalaya One Dish**

# EASY BEEF & PASTA

**Prep/Cook Time:** 20 minutes   *20 minutes or less!*

**1 pound boneless beef sirloin steak, ¾ inch thick**
**1 tablespoon vegetable oil**
**1 can (10¾ ounces) CAMPBELL'S Condensed Tomato Soup**
**½ cup water**
**1 bag (about 16 ounces) frozen side dish seasoned pasta and vegetable combination**

**1** Slice beef into very thin strips.

**2** In medium skillet over medium-high heat, heat oil. Add beef and cook until beef is browned and juices evaporate, stirring often.

**3** Add soup, water and vegetable combination. Heat to a boil. Reduce heat to low. Cover and cook 5 minutes or until beef and vegetables are done, stirring occasionally.                    *Serves 4*

*For easier slicing, place beef in the freezer for 45 to 60 minutes until it is partially frozen, then cut it into very thin slices.*

**Top to bottom: Chili Chicken Pasta Topper (page 33) and Easy Beef & Pasta**

# COUNTRY HERBED CHICKEN & VEGETABLES

**Prep Time:** 5 minutes     **Cook Time:** 25 minutes

> 1 tablespoon vegetable oil
> 1 pound skinless, boneless chicken breasts, cut up
> 1 can (10¾ ounces) CAMPBELL'S Condensed Cream of Chicken with Herbs Soup
> ½ cup milk
> 1 bag (16 ounces) frozen vegetable combination (broccoli, cauliflower, carrots)

**1** In medium skillet over medium-high heat, heat oil. Add chicken and cook until browned, stirring often. Set chicken aside. Pour off fat.

**2** Add soup, milk and vegetables. Heat to a boil. Return chicken to pan. Reduce heat to low. Cover and cook 10 minutes or until vegetables are tender.                    *Serves 4*

 *Substitute your favorite frozen vegetable combination for the broccoli, cauliflower and carrots combo called for here.*

**Top to bottom: Herb Roasted Chicken & Potatoes (page 65) and Country Herbed Chicken & Vegetables**

# SHORTCUT STROGANOFF

**Prep Time:** 5 minutes    **Cook Time:** 30 minutes

> 1 pound boneless beef sirloin steak, ¾ inch thick
> 1 tablespoon vegetable oil
> 1 can (10¾ ounces) CAMPBELL'S Condensed Cream of
>     Mushroom Soup *or* 98% Fat Free Cream of
>     Mushroom Soup
> 1 can (10½ ounces) CAMPBELL'S Condensed Beef Broth
> 1 cup water
> 2 teaspoons Worcestershire sauce
> 3 cups *uncooked* corkscrew pasta
> ½ cup sour cream

**1** Slice beef into very thin strips.

**2** In medium skillet over medium-high heat, heat oil. Add beef and cook until beef is browned and juices evaporate, stirring often.

**3** Add soup, broth, water and Worcestershire. Heat to a boil. Stir in pasta. Reduce heat to medium. Cook 15 minutes or until pasta is done, stirring often. Stir in sour cream. Heat through.

*Serves 4*

Top to bottom: Beef & Broccoli (page 32)
and Shortcut Stroganoff

# BEEF & BROCCOLI

*(photo on page 31)*

**Prep/Cook Time:** 25 minutes

- **1 pound boneless beef sirloin *or* top round steak, ¾ inch thick**
- **1 tablespoon vegetable oil**
- **1 can (10¾ ounces) CAMPBELL'S Condensed Tomato Soup**
- **3 tablespoons soy sauce**
- **1 tablespoon vinegar**
- **1 teaspoon garlic powder**
- **¼ teaspoon crushed red pepper (optional)**
- **3 cups fresh *or* thawed frozen broccoli flowerets**
- **4 cups hot cooked rice**

**1** Slice beef into very thin strips.

**2** In medium skillet over medium-high heat, heat oil. Add beef and stir-fry until browned and juices evaporate.

**3** Add soup, soy sauce, vinegar, garlic powder and pepper. Heat to a boil. Reduce heat to medium. Add broccoli and cook until tender-crisp, stirring occasionally. Serve over rice.     *Serves 4*

 *To thaw broccoli, microwave on HIGH 3 minutes.*

# CHILI CHICKEN PASTA TOPPER

*(photo on page 27)*

**Prep/Cook Time:** 20 minutes          *20 minutes or less!*

- 1 tablespoon vegetable oil
- 1 pound skinless, boneless chicken breasts, cubed
- 1 can (10¾ ounces) CAMPBELL'S Condensed Cream of Chicken with Herbs Soup
- ½ cup milk
- 2 tablespoons grated Parmesan cheese
- 1 teaspoon chili powder
- ½ teaspoon garlic powder
- 4 cups hot cooked corkscrew pasta (about 3 cups uncooked)

**1** In medium skillet over medium-high heat, heat oil. Add chicken and cook until browned, stirring often.

**2** Add soup, milk, cheese, chili powder and garlic powder and cook through, stirring often. Serve over pasta.          *Serves 4*

*When a recipe will be served over pasta or rice, save time by heating the cooking water while you're preparing the recipe. It'll be ready when you are!*

# *Campbell's*®

# Restaurant Style at Home

## ASIAN CHICKEN STIR-FRY

**Prep/Cook Time:** 20 minutes    *20 minutes or less!*

- 1 tablespoon vegetable oil
- 1 pound skinless, boneless chicken breasts, cut into strips
- 1 can (10¾ ounces) CAMPBELL'S Condensed Golden Mushroom Soup
- 3 tablespoons soy sauce
- 1 teaspoon garlic powder
- 1 bag (16 ounces) any frozen vegetable combination, thawed
- 4 cups hot cooked rice

**1** In medium skillet over medium-high heat, heat oil. Add chicken and stir-fry until browned and juices evaporate.

**2** Add soup, soy sauce and garlic powder. Heat to a boil. Reduce heat to medium. Add vegetables and cook until vegetables are tender-crisp, stirring often. Serve over rice.    *Serves 4*

**Asian Chicken Stir-Fry**

# CHICKEN QUESADILLAS & FIESTA RICE

*20 minutes or less!*

> 1 pound skinless, boneless chicken breasts, cubed
> 1 can (10¾ ounces) CAMPBELL'S Condensed Cheddar
>    Cheese Soup
> ½ cup PACE Thick & Chunky Salsa *or* Picante Sauce
>    (Medium)
> 10 flour tortillas (8-inch)
>    Fiesta Rice*

1 Preheat oven to 425°F.

2 In medium nonstick skillet over medium-high heat, cook chicken 5 minutes or until no longer pink and juices evaporate, stirring often. Add soup and salsa. Heat to a boil, stirring occasionally.

3 Place tortillas on 2 baking sheets. Top **half** of each tortilla with **about ⅓ cup** soup mixture. Spread to within ½ inch of edge. Moisten edges of tortilla with water. Fold over and press edges together.

4 Bake 5 minutes or until hot.                          *Serves 4*

**\*Fiesta Rice:** In saucepan heat 1 can CAMPBELL'S Condensed Chicken Broth, ½ cup water and ½ cup PACE Thick & Chunky Salsa *or* Picante Sauce to a boil. Stir in 2 cups *uncooked* Minute® Original Rice. Cover and remove from heat. Let stand 5 minutes.

Chicken Quesadillas & Fiesta Rice

# PAN ROASTED
# VEGETABLE & CHICKEN PIZZA

**Prep Time:** 20 minutes    **Cook Time:** 12 minutes

> Vegetable cooking spray
> ¾ pound skinless, boneless chicken breasts, cubed
> 3 cups cut-up vegetables*
> ⅛ teaspoon garlic powder *or* 1 clove garlic, minced
> 1 can (10¾ ounces) CAMPBELL'S Condensed Cream of Mushroom Soup *or* 98% Fat Free Cream of Mushroom Soup
> 1 Italian bread shell (12-inch)
> 1 cup shredded Monterey Jack cheese (4 ounces)

**1** Spray medium skillet with vegetable cooking spray and heat over medium-high heat 1 minute. Add chicken and cook 10 minutes or until browned, stirring often. Set chicken aside.

**2** Remove pan from heat. Spray with cooking spray. Reduce heat to medium. Add vegetables and garlic powder. Cook until tender-crisp. Add soup. Return chicken to pan. Heat through.

**3** Spread chicken mixture over shell to within ¼ inch of edge. Top with cheese. Bake at 450°F. for 12 minutes or until cheese is melted.                                          *Serves 4*

*Use a combination of sliced zucchini, red *or* green pepper cut into 2-inch long strips, and thinly sliced onion.

**Top to bottom: Creamy Chicken Risotto (page 40) and Pan Roasted Vegetable & Chicken Pizza**

# CREAMY CHICKEN RISOTTO

*(photo on page 39)*

**Prep Time:** 10 minutes    **Cook Time:** 35 minutes

> 1 tablespoon vegetable oil
> 1 pound skinless, boneless chicken breasts, cut up
> 1 can (10¾ ounces) CAMPBELL'S Condensed Cream of Mushroom with Roasted Garlic Soup
> 1 can (10½ ounces) CAMPBELL'S Condensed Chicken Broth
> ¾ cup water
> 1 small carrot, shredded (about ⅓ cup)
> 2 medium green onions, sliced (about ¼ cup)
> 1 tablespoon grated Parmesan cheese
> 1 cup *uncooked* regular long-grain white rice

**1** In medium skillet over medium-high heat, heat oil. Add chicken and cook until browned, stirring often.

**2** Add soup, broth, water, carrot, onions and cheese. Heat to a boil. Stir in rice. Reduce heat to low. Cover and cook 25 minutes until chicken and rice are done and most of liquid is absorbed, stirring occasionally.

*Serves 4*

# ORANGE BEEF

(photo on page 43)

**Prep Time:** 10 minutes     **Cook Time:** 20 minutes

> **1 pound boneless beef sirloin steak, ¾ inch thick**
> **2 tablespoons vegetable oil**
> **1 medium green pepper, cut into 2-inch long strips**
>     **(about 1½ cups)**
> **1 medium onion, sliced (about ½ cup)**
> **1 can (10¾ ounces) CAMPBELL'S Condensed Tomato**
>     **Soup**
> **¼ cup orange juice**
> **2 tablespoons soy sauce**
> **1 tablespoon vinegar**
> **1 teaspoon garlic powder**
> **4 cups hot cooked rice**

**1** Slice beef into very thin strips.

**2** In medium skillet over medium-high heat, heat **half** the oil. Add beef and stir-fry until beef is browned and juices evaporate.

**3** Reduce heat to medium. Add remaining oil. Add pepper and onion and cook until tender crisp.

**4** Add soup, orange juice, soy sauce, vinegar and garlic powder. Heat through, stirring occasionally. Serve over rice.     *Serves 4*

# EASY BEEF TERIYAKI

**Prep Time:** 10 minutes     **Cook Time:** 20 minutes

- **1 pound boneless beef sirloin steak, ¾ inch thick**
- **1 tablespoon vegetable oil**
- **1 can (10¾ ounces) CAMPBELL'S Condensed Golden Mushroom Soup**
- **2 tablespoons soy sauce**
- **1 tablespoon packed brown sugar**
- **1 bag (about 16 ounces) frozen Oriental stir-fry vegetables**
- **4 cups hot cooked rice**

**1** Slice beef into very thin strips.

**2** In medium skillet over medium-high heat, heat oil. Add beef and stir-fry until beef is browned and juices evaporate.

**3** Add soup, soy sauce and sugar. Heat to a boil. Reduce heat to medium. Add vegetables. Cover and cook 5 minutes until vegetables are tender-crisp, stirring occasionally. Serve over rice.                    *Serves 4*

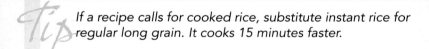

*If a recipe calls for cooked rice, substitute instant rice for regular long grain. It cooks 15 minutes faster.*

**Top to bottom: Orange Beef (page 41) and Easy Beef Teriyaki**

# CHEESESTEAK POCKETS

*20 minutes or less!*

1 tablespoon vegetable oil
1. medium onion, sliced (about ½ cup)
1 package (14 ounces) frozen beef *or* chicken sandwich
    steaks, cut into 8 pieces
1 can (10¾ ounces) CAMPBELL'S Condensed Cheddar
    Cheese Soup
1 jar (about 4½ ounces) sliced mushrooms, drained
4 pita breads (6-inch), cut in half, forming two pockets
    each

**1** In medium skillet over medium-high heat, heat oil. Add onion
and cook until tender. Add sandwich steaks and cook 5 minutes
or until browned, stirring often. Pour off fat.

**2** Add soup and mushrooms. Heat to a boil. Reduce heat to low
and heat through. Spoon meat mixture into pita halves.

*Makes 4 sandwiches*

Top to bottom: **Buffalo-Style Burger (page 46)
and Cheesesteak Pockets**

# BUFFALO–STYLE BURGERS

*(photo on page 45)*

**Prep/Cook Time:** 20 minutes      *20 minutes or less!*

> 1 pound ground beef
> 1 can (10¾ ounces) CAMPBELL'S Condensed Tomato
>   Soup
> ⅛ teaspoon hot pepper sauce
> 4 hamburger rolls, split and toasted
> ½ cup crumbled blue cheese (about 4 ounces)

**1** Shape beef into 4 patties, ½ inch thick.

**2** In medium skillet over medium-high heat, cook patties until browned. Set patties aside. Pour off fat.

**3** Add soup and hot pepper sauce. Heat to a boil. Return patties to pan. Reduce heat to low. Cover and cook 10 minutes or until patties are no longer pink (160°F.).

**4** Place patties on 4 roll halves. Top with cheese and remaining roll halves.                    *Makes 4 sandwiches*

# MONTEREY CHICKEN FAJITAS

*(photo on page 49)*

**Prep Time:** 10 minutes    **Cook Time:** 20 minutes

2 tablespoons vegetable oil
1 pound skinless, boneless chicken breasts, cut into strips
1 medium green pepper, cut into 2-inch long strips
     (about 1½ cups)
1 medium onion, sliced (about ½ cup)
1 can (10¾ ounces) CAMPBELL'S Condensed Cream of
     Mushroom Soup *or* 98% Fat Free Cream of
     Mushroom Soup
½ cup PACE Thick & Chunky Salsa *or* Picante Sauce
8 flour tortillas (8-inch)
1 cup shredded Monterey Jack cheese (4 ounces)

1 In medium skillet over medium-high heat, heat *half* the oil. Add chicken and cook until browned and juices evaporate, stirring often. Set chicken aside.

2 Reduce heat to medium. Add remaining oil. Add pepper and onion and cook until tender-crisp. Pour off fat.

3 Add soup and salsa. Heat to a boil. Return chicken to pan and heat through. Spoon *about ½ cup* chicken mixture down center of each tortilla. Top with cheese and additional salsa. Fold tortilla around filling.                                    *Serves 4*

# SOUTHWESTERN CHICKEN & PEPPER WRAPS

**Prep Time:** 10 minutes    **Cook/Stand Time:** 25 minutes

2 tablespoons vegetable oil
1 pound skinless, boneless chicken breasts, cut into strips
1 medium red pepper, cut into 2-inch long strips (about 1½ cups)
1 medium green pepper, cut into 2-inch long strips (about 1½ cups)
1 small onion, sliced (about ¼ cup)
1 can (10¾ ounces) CAMPBELL'S Condensed Golden Mushroom Soup
1 cup water
1 cup black beans, rinsed and drained (optional)
1 cup *uncooked* Minute® Original Rice
8 flour tortillas (8-inch)

**1** In medium skillet over medium-high heat, heat *half* the oil. Add chicken and cook 10 minutes or until no longer pink and juices evaporate, stirring often.

**2** Reduce heat to medium. Add remaining oil. Add peppers and onion and cook until tender-crisp, stirring often.

**3** Add soup, water and beans. Heat to a boil. Stir in rice. Cover and remove from heat. Let stand 5 minutes.

**4** Spoon *¾ cup* chicken mixture down center of each tortilla. Fold tortilla around filling.                                                          *Serves 4*

**Top to bottom: Monterey Chicken Fajita (page 47) and Southwestern Chicken & Pepper Wrap**

# *Campbell's*®

# Quick-Fix Oven Wonders

## ONE-DISH CHICKEN & RICE BAKE

**Prep Time:** 5 minutes     **Cook Time:** 45 minutes

    1 can (10¾ ounces) CAMPBELL'S Condensed Cream of
        Mushroom Soup *or* 98% Fat Free Cream of
        Mushroom Soup
    1 cup water*
    ¾ cup *uncooked* regular white rice
    ¼ teaspoon paprika
    ¼ teaspoon pepper
    4 skinless, boneless chicken breast halves (about
        1 pound)

**1** In 2-quart shallow baking dish mix soup, water, rice, paprika and pepper. Place chicken on rice mixture. Sprinkle with additional paprika and pepper. **Cover.**

**2** Bake at 375°F. for 45 minutes or until chicken is no longer pink and rice is done.        *Serves 4*

*For creamier rice, increase water to 1⅓ cups.

**Top to bottom: One-Dish Chicken & Stuffing Bake (page 57) and One-Dish Chicken & Rice Bake**

# SIMPLY DELICIOUS MEAT LOAF

**Prep Time:** 5 minutes     **Cook Time:** 1 hour 5 minutes

> **1½ pounds ground beef**
> **½ cup Italian-seasoned dry bread crumbs**
> **1 egg, beaten**
> **1 can (10¾ ounces) CAMPBELL'S Condensed Golden Mushroom Soup**
> **¼ cup water**

**1** Mix beef, bread crumbs and egg *thoroughly*. In medium baking pan shape *firmly* into 8- by 4-inch loaf.

**2** Bake at 350°F. for 30 minutes. Spread ½ *can* soup over top of meat loaf. Bake 30 minutes more or until meat loaf is no longer pink (160°F.).

**3** In small saucepan mix *2 tablespoons* drippings, remaining soup and water. Heat through. Serve with meat loaf.          *Serves 6*

**Left to right: Parmesan Potatoes (page 81) and Simply Delicious Meat Loaf**

# FIESTA CHICKEN & RICE BAKE

**Prep Time:** 5 minutes    **Cook Time:** 45 minutes

 1 can (10¾ ounces) **CAMPBELL'S Condensed Cream of Chicken Soup** *or* **98% Fat Free Cream of Chicken Soup**
 1 cup **PACE Thick & Chunky Salsa** *or* **Picante Sauce**
 ½ cup water
 1 cup whole kernel corn
 ¾ cup *uncooked* regular white rice
 4 skinless, boneless chicken breast halves (about 1 pound)
  Paprika
 ½ cup shredded Cheddar cheese (2 ounces)

**1** In 2-quart shallow baking dish mix soup, salsa, water, corn and rice. Place chicken on rice mixture. Sprinkle paprika over chicken. **Cover.**

**2** Bake at 375°F. for 45 minutes or until chicken is no longer pink and rice is done. Sprinkle with cheese.                    *Serves 4*

**Top to bottom: Asian Chicken & Rice Bake (page 56) and Fiesta Chicken & Rice Bake**

# ASIAN CHICKEN & RICE BAKE

*(photo on page 55)*

**Prep Time:** 5 minutes    **Cook Time:** 45 minutes

> ¾ cup *uncooked* regular white rice
> 4 skinless, boneless chicken breast halves (about 1 pound)
> 1 can (10¾ ounces) CAMPBELL'S Condensed Golden Mushroom Soup
> ¾ cup water
> 2 tablespoons soy sauce
> 2 tablespoons cider vinegar
> 2 tablespoons honey
> 1 teaspoon garlic powder
> Paprika

**1** Spread rice in 2-quart shallow baking dish. Place chicken on rice.

**2** Mix soup, water, soy sauce, vinegar, honey and garlic powder. Pour over chicken. Sprinkle with paprika. **Cover**.

**3** Bake at 375°F. for 45 minutes or until chicken is no longer pink and rice is done.                    *Serves 4*

**Sesame Asian Chicken & Rice Bake:** Sprinkle with toasted sesame seeds after baking.

# ONE–DISH CHICKEN & STUFFING BAKE

*(photo on page 51)*

**Prep Time:** 10 minutes    **Cook Time:** 30 minutes

1¼ cups boiling water
4 tablespoons margarine *or* butter, melted
4 cups PEPPERIDGE FARM Herb Seasoned Stuffing
4 to 6 skinless, boneless chicken breast halves (about
    1 to 1½ pounds)
Paprika
1 can (10¾ ounces) CAMPBELL'S Condensed Cream of
    Mushroom Soup *or* 98% Fat Free Cream of
    Mushroom Soup
⅓ cup milk
1 tablespoon chopped fresh parsley *or* 1 teaspoon dried
    parsley flakes

**1** Mix water and margarine. Add stuffing. Mix lightly.

**2** Spoon stuffing across center of 3-quart shallow baking dish, leaving space on both sides for chicken. Arrange chicken on each side of stuffing. Sprinkle paprika over chicken.

**3** Mix soup, milk and parsley. Pour over chicken.

**4** **Cover.** Bake at 400°F. for 30 minutes or until chicken is no longer pink.     *Serves 4 to 6*

# GARLIC MASHED POTATOES & BEEF BAKE

**Prep Time:** 10 minutes    **Cook Time:** 20 minutes

> **1 pound ground beef**
> **1 can (10¾ ounces) CAMPBELL'S Condensed Cream of Mushroom with Roasted Garlic Soup**
> **1 tablespoon Worcestershire sauce**
> **1 bag (16 ounces) frozen vegetable combination (broccoli, cauliflower, carrots), thawed**
> **3 cups hot mashed potatoes**

**1** In medium skillet over medium-high heat, cook beef until browned, stirring to separate meat. Pour off fat.

**2** In 2-quart shallow baking dish mix beef, ½ **can** soup, Worcestershire and vegetables.

**3** Stir remaining soup into potatoes. Spoon potato mixture over beef mixture. Bake at 400°F. for 20 minutes or until hot.

*Serves 4*

*Tip* To thaw vegetables, microwave on HIGH 3 minutes.

**Garlic Mashed Potatoes & Beef Bake**

# HAM & BROCCOLI SHORTCUT STROMBOLI

**Prep Time:** 10 minutes    **Cook Time:** 20 minutes

> 1 package (10 ounces) refrigerated pizza dough
> 1 can (10¾ ounces) CAMPBELL'S Condensed Cream of Celery Soup
> 1 cup cooked chopped broccoli
> 2 cups cubed cooked ham
> 1 cup shredded Cheddar cheese (4 ounces)

**1** Preheat oven to 400°F. Unroll dough onto greased baking sheet. Set aside.

**2** Mix soup, broccoli and ham. Spread soup mixture down center of dough. Top with cheese. Fold long sides of dough over filling and pinch and seal. Pinch short sides to seal.

**3** Bake 20 minutes or until golden brown. Slice and serve.

*Serves 4*

**Roast Beef & Bean Shortcut Stromboli:** Substitute 1 can CAMPBELL'S Condensed Cream of Mushroom Soup, 1 cup cut green beans and 2 cups cubed cooked roast beef for Cream of Celery Soup, broccoli and ham.

**Chicken & Vegetable Shortcut Stromboli:** Substitute 1 can CAMPBELL'S Condensed Cream of Chicken Soup, 1 cup mixed vegetables and 2 cups cubed cooked chicken *or* turkey for Cream of Celery Soup, broccoli and ham.

**Top to bottom: Cod Vera Cruz (page 64) and Ham & Broccoli Shortcut Stromboli**

# E-Z CHICKEN TORTILLA BAKE

**Prep Time:** 10 minutes    **Cook Time:** 30 minutes

> 1 can (10¾ ounces) CAMPBELL'S Condensed Tomato Soup
> 1 cup PACE Thick & Chunky Salsa *or* Picante Sauce
> ½ cup milk
> 2 cups cubed cooked chicken *or* turkey
> 8 corn tortillas (6- *or* 8-inch), cut into 1-inch pieces
> 1 cup shredded Cheddar cheese (4 ounces)

**1** In 2-quart shallow baking dish mix soup, salsa, milk, chicken, tortillas and *half* the cheese. **Cover.**

**2** Bake at 400°F. for 30 minutes or until hot. Top with remaining cheese.                                    *Serves 4*

# SLOPPY JOE PIZZA

**Prep Time:** 10 minutes    **Cook Time:** 12 minutes

> ¾ pound ground beef
> 1 can (10¾ ounces) CAMPBELL'S Condensed Tomato Soup
> 1 Italian bread shell (12-inch)
> 1½ cups shredded Cheddar cheese (6 ounces)

**1** In medium skillet over medium-high heat, cook beef until browned, stirring to separate meat. Pour off fat.

**2** Add soup. Heat through. Spread beef mixture over shell to within ¼ inch of edge. Top with cheese. Bake at 450°F. for 12 minutes or until cheese is melted.                    *Serves 4*

**Top to bottom: E-Z Chicken Tortilla Bake, 3-Cheese Pasta Bake (page 64) and Sloppy Joe Pizza**

# COD VERA CRUZ

*(photo on page 61)*

**Prep Time:** 10 minutes    **Cook Time:** 20 minutes

  1 pound fresh *or* thawed frozen cod *or* haddock fillets
  1 can (10¾ ounces) CAMPBELL'S Condensed Tomato Soup
  1 can (10½ ounces) CAMPBELL'S Condensed Chicken Broth
  ⅓ cup PACE Thick & Chunky Salsa *or* Picante Sauce
  1 tablespoon lime juice
  2 teaspoons chopped fresh cilantro
  1 teaspoon dried oregano leaves, crushed
  ⅛ teaspoon garlic powder *or* 1 clove garlic, minced
  4 cups hot cooked rice

**1** Place fish in 2-quart shallow baking dish.

**2** Mix soup, broth, salsa, lime juice, cilantro, oregano and garlic powder. Pour over fish. Bake at 400°F. for 20 minutes or until fish flakes easily when tested with a fork. Serve over rice.

*Serves 4*

# 3-CHEESE PASTA BAKE

*(photo on page 63)*

**Prep Time:** 10 minutes    **Cook Time:** 20 minutes

  1 can (10¾ ounces) CAMPBELL'S Condensed Cream of
       Mushroom Soup *or* 98% Fat Free Cream of
       Mushroom Soup
  1 package (8 ounces) shredded 2-cheese blend (2 cups)
  ⅓ cup grated Parmesan cheese
  1 cup milk
  ¼ teaspoon pepper
  4 cups cooked corkscrew pasta (about 3 cups uncooked)

In 1½-quart casserole mix soup, cheeses, milk and pepper. Stir in pasta. Bake at 400°F. for 20 minutes or until hot.     *Serves 4*

# HERB ROASTED CHICKEN & POTATOES

*(photo on page 29)*

**Prep Time:** 10 minutes     **Cook Time:** 30 minutes

    1 large plastic oven bag
    4 skinless, boneless chicken breast halves (about
        1 pound)
    8 small red potatoes, cut into quarters (about 1 pound)
    1 can (10¾ ounces) CAMPBELL'S Condensed Cream of
        Chicken with Herbs Soup
    ¼ cup water
    ½ teaspoon garlic powder
        Chopped fresh parsley for garnish

**1** Preheat oven to 375°F. Prepare oven bag according to package directions using **1 tablespoon all-purpose flour.** Place chicken and potatoes in oven bag.

**2** In a small bowl mix soup, water and garlic powder. Pour into oven bag. Close bag with nylon tie. Cut 6 (½-inch) slits in top of bag.

**3** Bake at 375°F. for 30 minutes or until chicken is no longer pink and potatoes are done. Garnish with parsley.     *Serves 4*

*Tip*

*Coating the inside of the oven bag with flour protects it from bursting during baking.*

# EASY CHICKEN POT PIE

**Prep Time:** 5 minutes    **Cook Time:** 30 minutes

- 1 can (10¾ ounces) CAMPBELL'S Condensed Cream of Chicken with Herbs Soup
- 1 package (about 9 ounces) frozen mixed vegetables, thawed
- 1 cup cubed cooked chicken *or* turkey
- ½ cup milk
- 1 egg
- 1 cup all-purpose baking mix

**1** Preheat oven to 400°F. In 9-inch pie plate mix soup, vegetables and chicken.

**2** Mix milk, egg and baking mix. Pour over chicken mixture. Bake 30 minutes or until golden brown.                *Serves 4*

**No Guilt Chicken Pot Pie:** Substitute 1 can CAMPBELL'S Condensed 98% Fat Free Cream of Chicken Soup for Cream of Chicken with Herbs Soup and 1 cup reduced fat baking mix for all-purpose baking mix.

*For 1 cup cubed cooked chicken: In medium saucepan over medium heat, in 3 to 4 cups simmering water, cook ½ pound skinless, boneless chicken breasts 5 minutes or until chicken is no longer pink (170°F.).*

**No Guilt Chicken Pot Pie (variation of Easy Chicken Pot Pie)**

# CHICKEN FLORENTINE LASAGNA

**Prep Time:** 10 minutes     **Cook/Stand Time:** 1 hour 5 minutes

> **2 cans (10¾ ounces *each*) CAMPBELL'S Condensed Cream of Chicken with Herbs Soup**
> **2 cups milk**
> **1 egg**
> **1 container (15 ounces) ricotta cheese**
> **6 *uncooked* lasagna noodles**
> **1 package (about 10 ounces) frozen chopped spinach, thawed and well drained**
> **2 cups cubed cooked chicken *or* turkey**
> **2 cups shredded Cheddar cheese (8 ounces)**

**1** Mix soup and milk until smooth. Set aside.

**2** Mix egg and ricotta. Set aside.

**3** In 3-quart shallow baking dish, spread *1 cup* soup mixture. Top with *3 uncooked* lasagna noodles, ricotta mixture, spinach, chicken, *1 cup* Cheddar cheese and *1 cup* soup mixture. Top with remaining *3 uncooked* lasagna noodles and remaining soup mixture. **Cover.**

**4** Bake at 375°F. for 1 hour. Uncover and top with remaining Cheddar cheese. Let stand 5 minutes.               *Serves 6*

---

*Tip*

*To thaw spinach, microwave on HIGH 3 minutes, breaking apart with a fork halfway through heating.*

**Chicken Florentine Lasagna**

# FLASH ROASTED
# CRISPY RANCH CHICKEN

**Prep Time:** 5 minutes    **Cook Time:** 20 minutes

1 can (10¾ ounces) CAMPBELL'S Condensed Cream of
  Chicken Soup *or* 98% Fat Free Cream of Chicken
  Soup
½ cup milk
1 envelope (1 ounce) ranch salad dressing mix
4 skinless, boneless chicken breast halves (about
  1 pound)
1½ cups finely crushed tortilla chips
2 tablespoons margarine *or* butter, melted

**1** In shallow dish mix soup, milk and dressing mix. Reserve *1 cup* for sauce.

**2** Dip chicken into soup mixture. Coat with tortilla chips.

**3** Place chicken on greased baking sheet. Drizzle with margarine. Bake at 400°F. for 20 minutes or until chicken is no longer pink.

**4** In small saucepan over medium heat, heat reserved soup mixture to a boil. Serve with chicken.                    *Serves 4*

**Left to right: Creamy Vegetable Medley (page 81)
and Flash Roasted Crispy Ranch Chicken**

# CORNBREAD CHICKEN POT PIE

**Prep Time:** 10 minutes     **Cook Time:** 30 minutes

> 1 can (10¾ ounces) CAMPBELL'S Condensed Cream of Chicken Soup *or* 98% Fat Free Cream of Chicken Soup
> 1 can (about 8 ounces) whole kernel corn, drained
> 2 cups cubed cooked chicken *or* turkey
> 1 package (8½ ounces) corn muffin mix
> ¾ cup milk
> 1 egg
> ½ cup shredded Cheddar cheese (2 ounces)

**1** Preheat oven to 400°F. In 9-inch pie plate mix soup, corn and chicken.

**2** Mix muffin mix, milk and egg. Pour over chicken mixture. Bake for 30 minutes or until golden. Sprinkle with cheese.

*Serves 4*

**Cornbread Chicken Chili Pot Pie:** In Step 1 add 1 can (about 4 ounces) chopped green chilies, drained, with the corn.

*Don't waste time shredding or grating cheese. Buy packaged shredded/grated cheese at the store. You'll save at least 5 minutes and you won't have to clean the grater!*

Cornbread Chicken Pot Pie

# *Campbell's*®

# Simple Sides

## GREEN BEAN BAKE

**Prep Time:** 10 minutes    **Cook Time:** 30 minutes

>    1 can (10¾ ounces) CAMPBELL'S Condensed Cream of
>       Mushroom Soup *or* 98% Fat Free Cream of
>       Mushroom Soup
>    ½ cup milk
>    1 teaspoon soy sauce
>       Dash pepper
>    4 cups cooked cut green beans*
>    1 can (2.8 ounces) French's® French Fried Onions
>       (1⅓ cups)

**1** In 1½-quart casserole mix soup, milk, soy sauce, pepper, beans and ½ *can* onions.

**2** Bake at 350°F. for 25 minutes or until hot.

**3** Stir. Sprinkle remaining onions over bean mixture. Bake 5 minutes more or until onions are golden.                    *Serves 6*

*Use 1 bag (16 to 20 ounces) frozen green beans, 2 packages (9 ounces each) frozen green beans, 2 cans (about 16 ounces each) green beans or about 1½ pounds fresh green beans for this recipe.

**Green Bean Bake**

# CHEESY BROCCOLI

**Prep/Cook Time:** 10 minutes    *20 minutes or less!*

  **1 can (10¾ ounces) CAMPBELL'S Condensed Cheddar
    Cheese Soup**
  **¼ cup milk**
  **4 cups frozen broccoli cuts**

**1** In 2-quart microwave-safe casserole mix soup and milk. Add
broccoli.

**2** Cover and microwave on HIGH 8 minutes or until broccoli is
tender-crisp, stirring once during heating.            *Serves 4*

# CHEESE FRIES

**Prep/Cook Time:** 20 minutes    *20 minutes or less!*

  **1 bag (32 ounces) frozen French fried potatoes**
  **1 can (10¾ ounces) CAMPBELL'S Condensed Cheddar
    Cheese Soup**

**1** On baking sheet bake potatoes according to package
directions.

**2** Push potatoes into pile in center of baking sheet. Stir soup in
can and spoon over potatoes.

**3** Bake 3 minutes more or until soup is hot.            *Serves 6*

**Nacho Cheese Fries:** Substitute CAMPBELL'S Condensed
Fiesta Nacho Cheese Soup for the Cheddar Cheese Soup.

**Top to bottom: Cheese Fries and
Cheesy Broccoli**

# CHEDDARY POUCH POTATOES

**Prep Time:** 5 minutes     **Cook Time:** 25 minutes

> 1 can (10¾ ounces) CAMPBELL'S Condensed Cheddar
>     Cheese Soup
> ¼ cup milk
> ½ teaspoon garlic powder
> ¼ teaspoon onion powder
> 4 cups frozen steak fries
>     Paprika

**1** In large bowl mix soup, milk, garlic powder and onion powder.
Stir in potatoes.

**2** Cut four 14-inch squares of heavy-duty aluminum foil. Spoon
*1 cup* soup mixture onto each square, arranging potatoes to
make a single layer. Sprinkle with paprika. Bring up sides of foil
and double fold. Double fold ends to make packet.

**3** Place potato packets on grill rack over medium-hot coals. Grill
25 minutes or until potatoes are tender.          *Serves 4*

**Cheddary Oven Pouch Potatoes:** In Step 3, on baking sheet
bake packets at 350°F. for 25 minutes.

**Top to bottom: Cheddar Broccoli Bake (page 80)
and Cheddary Pouch Potatoes**

# CHEDDAR BROCCOLI BAKE

*(photo on page 79)*

**Prep Time:** 10 minutes     **Cook Time:** 30 minutes

> 1 can (10¾ ounces) CAMPBELL'S Condensed Cheddar
>     Cheese Soup
> ½ cup milk
>     Dash pepper
> 4 cups cooked broccoli cuts
> 1 can (2.8 ounces) French's® French Fried Onions
>     (1⅓ cups)

**1** In 1½-quart casserole mix soup, milk, pepper, broccoli and
½ *can* onions.

**2** Bake at 350°F. for 25 minutes or until hot.

**3** Stir. Sprinkle remaining onions over broccoli mixture. Bake 5
minutes more or until onions are golden.          *Serves 6*

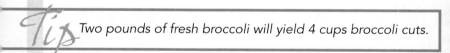

*Two pounds of fresh broccoli will yield 4 cups broccoli cuts.*

# PARMESAN POTATOES

*(photo on page 53)*

**Prep Time:** 5 minutes    **Cook Time:** 45 minutes

   1 can (10¾ ounces) CAMPBELL'S Condensed Cheddar
       Cheese Soup
   ½ cup milk
   ½ cup grated Parmesan cheese
   ¼ teaspoon pepper
   4 medium white potatoes, cut in 1-inch pieces (about
       4 cups)
   1 can (2.8 ounces) French's® French Fried Onions
       (1⅓ cups)

**1** In greased shallow 2-quart baking dish mix soup, milk, cheese
and pepper. Stir in potatoes and ½ *can* onions.

**2** Bake at 400°F. for 40 minutes or until potatoes are tender.
Sprinkle remaining onions over potatoes. Bake 5 minutes more
or until onions are golden.                                    *Serves 4*

# CREAMY VEGETABLE MEDLEY

*(photo on page 71)*

**Prep Time:** 15 minutes    **Cook Time:** 20 minutes

   1 can (10¾ ounces) CAMPBELL'S Condensed Cream of
       Celery Soup *or* 98% Fat Free Cream of Celery Soup
   ½ cup milk
   2 cups broccoli flowerets
   2 medium carrots, sliced (about 1 cup)
   1 cup cauliflower flowerets

**1** In medium saucepan mix soup, milk, broccoli, carrots and
cauliflower. Over medium heat, heat to a boil.

**2** Reduce heat to low. Cover and cook 15 minutes or until
vegetables are tender, stirring occasionally.              *Serves 6*

# Campbell's®

# Slow Cooker Creations

## GOLDEN MUSHROOM PORK & APPLES

**Prep Time:** 10 minutes    **Cook Time:** 8 to 9 hours

  2 cans (10¾ ounces *each*) CAMPBELL'S Condensed
      Golden Mushroom Soup
½ cup water
  1 tablespoon brown sugar
  1 tablespoon Worcestershire sauce
  1 teaspoon dried thyme leaves, crushed
  4 large Granny Smith apples, sliced (about 4 cups)
  2 large onions, sliced (about 2 cups)
  8 boneless pork chops, ¾ inch thick (about 2 pounds)

In slow cooker mix soup, water, brown sugar, Worcestershire
and thyme. Add apples, onions and pork. Cover and cook on
***low*** 8 to 9 hours or until pork is tender.              *Serves 8*

**Top to bottom: Savory Pot Roast (page 87)
and Golden Mushroom Pork & Apples**

# LEMON CHICKEN

**Prep Time:** 5 minutes    **Cook Time:** 7 to 8 hours

   2 cans (10¾ ounces *each*) CAMPBELL'S Condensed Cream of Chicken Soup *or* 98% Fat Free Cream of Chicken Soup
  ½ cup water
  ¼ cup lemon juice
   2 teaspoons Dijon-style mustard
 1½ teaspoons garlic powder
   8 large carrots, thickly sliced (about 6 cups)
   8 skinless, boneless chicken breast halves (about 2 pounds)
   8 cups hot cooked egg noodles
    Grated Parmesan cheese

**1** In slow cooker mix soup, water, lemon juice, mustard, garlic powder and carrots. Add chicken and turn to coat. Cover and cook on **low** 7 to 8 hours or until chicken is done.

**2** Serve over noodles. Sprinkle with cheese.    *Serves 8*

Top to bottom: Asian Tomato Beef (page 86) and Lemon Chicken

# ASIAN TOMATO BEEF

*(photo on page 85)*

**Prep Time:** 10 minutes    **Cook Time:** 7 to 8 hours and
15 minutes

   2 cans (10¾ ounces *each*) CAMPBELL'S Condensed
      Tomato Soup
   ⅓ cup soy sauce
   ⅓ cup vinegar
 1½ teaspoons garlic powder
   ¼ teaspoon pepper
   1 (3- to 3½-pound) boneless beef round steak, ¾ inch
      thick, cut into strips
   6 cups broccoli flowerets
   8 cups hot cooked rice

**1** In slow cooker mix soup, soy sauce, vinegar, garlic powder,
pepper and beef. Cover and cook on *low* 7 to 8 hours or until
beef is done.

**2** Stir. Arrange broccoli over beef. Cover and cook on *high*
15 minutes more or until tender-crisp. Serve over rice.

*Serves 8*

*No time to chop fresh produce? Buy bags of precut
vegetables—they work great in many recipes!*

# SAVORY POT ROAST

*(photo on page 83)*

**Prep Time:** 10 minutes    **Cook Time:** 8 to 9 hours

> 1 can (10¾ ounces) CAMPBELL'S Condensed Cream of
>   Mushroom Soup *or* 98% Fat Free Cream of
>   Mushroom Soup
> 1 pouch CAMPBELL'S Dry Onion Soup and Recipe Mix
> 6 medium potatoes, cut into 1-inch pieces (about 6 cups)
> 6 medium carrots, thickly sliced (about 3 cups)
> 1 (3½- to 4-pound) boneless chuck pot roast, trimmed

In slow cooker mix soup, soup mix, potatoes and carrots. Add
roast and turn to coat. Cover and cook on *low* 8 to 9 hours or
until roast and vegetables are done.                    *Serves 7 to 8*

# CREAMY CHICKEN & WILD RICE

*(photo on page 89)*

**Prep Time:** 5 minutes    **Cook Time:** 7 to 8 hours

> 2 cans (10¾ ounces *each*) CAMPBELL'S Condensed
>   Cream of Chicken Soup *or* 98% Fat Free Cream of
>   Chicken Soup
> 1½ cups water
> 1 package (6 ounces) seasoned long grain and wild
>   rice mix
> 4 large carrots, thickly sliced (about 3 cups)
> 8 skinless, boneless chicken breast halves (about
>   2 pounds)

In slow cooker mix soup, water, rice and carrots. Add chicken
and turn to coat. Cover and cook on *low* 7 to 8 hours or until
chicken and rice are done.                              *Serves 8*

# NACHO CHICKEN & RICE WRAPS

**Prep Time:** 5 minutes     **Cook Time:** 7 to 8 hours

  2 cans (10¾ ounces *each*) CAMPBELL'S Condensed
      Cheddar Cheese Soup
  1 cup water
  2 cups PACE Thick & Chunky Salsa *or* Picante Sauce
1¼ cups *uncooked* regular long-grain white rice
  2 pounds skinless, boneless chicken breasts, cut into
      cubes
 10 flour tortillas (10-inch)

**1** In slow cooker mix soup, water, salsa, rice and chicken. Cover
and cook on *low* 7 to 8 hours or until chicken and rice are
done.

**2** Spoon *about 1 cup* rice mixture down center of each tortilla.

**3** Fold opposite sides of tortilla over filling. Roll up from bottom.
Cut each wrap in half.                                    *Serves 10*

*Tip* *For firmer rice, substitute converted rice for regular.*

For information on purchasing the *Campbell's* Slow Cooker, please call
1-888-768-7766.

**Top to bottom: Creamy Chicken & Wild Rice (page 87)
and Nacho Chicken & Rice Wrap**

# *Campbell's*

# Quick Cooking Tips

■ To avoid last minute stress, take a few minutes to plan family menus in advance. Remember that *Campbell's* cookbooks are a great resource for quick homemade meal ideas!

■ Cut down on shopping time—keep CAMPBELL'S Condensed Soups on hand. You can make easy and delicious everyday meals with ingredients right from the pantry!

■ Feed the kids quickly with CAMPBELL'S Cheddar Cheese Soup! Just mix with cooked chicken and PACE Salsa for a great quesadilla filling, or pour over baked potatoes or nachos.

■ No more need to chop mushrooms or garlic! Just use CAMPBELL'S Cream of Mushroom with Roasted Garlic Soup to add delicious flavor instantly to meat, poultry, pasta or rice.

■ Stir your favorite CAMPBELL'S Condensed Soup into cooked instant rice for a savory side dish in no time!

- Double a recipe and freeze or refrigerate half for an instant meal later in the week.

- If a recipe calls for cooked pasta and vegetables, save time by cooking them together! Add the vegetables to the pasta partway through the cooking time.

- If a recipe calls for cooked pasta and time is short, use faster cooking pastas, such as angel hair or spaghetti.

- When a recipe calls for chicken strips, don't spend time slicing chicken breasts—buy chicken tenders instead.

- Save on cleanup time by portioning food right from the pot onto dinner plates. Call it restaurant-style!

- Freeze make-ahead dishes in freezer/microwave-safe containers for speedy reheating.

- Freeze leftovers in flat containers rather than deep ones. They will defrost faster.

- To defrost meat quickly and safely, use your microwave! (Be sure to follow the manufacturer's instructions for defrosting.)

- Save time by preparing your casserole in a baking dish that doubles as a serving dish—less cleanup!

- For side dishes and mix-ins, keep frozen vegetables on hand—they cook faster and keep longer than fresh vegetables!

# Recipe Index

# Product Index

# NOTES

# METRIC CONVERSION CHART

## VOLUME MEASUREMENTS (dry)

1/8 teaspoon = 0.5 mL
1/4 teaspoon = 1 mL
1/2 teaspoon = 2 mL
3/4 teaspoon = 4 mL
1 teaspoon = 5 mL
1 tablespoon = 15 mL
2 tablespoons = 30 mL
1/4 cup = 60 mL
1/3 cup = 75 mL
1/2 cup = 125 mL
2/3 cup = 150 mL
3/4 cup = 175 mL
1 cup = 250 mL
2 cups = 1 pint = 500 mL
3 cups = 750 mL
4 cups = 1 quart = 1 L

## VOLUME MEASUREMENTS (fluid)

1 fluid ounce (2 tablespoons) = 30 mL
4 fluid ounces (1/2 cup) = 125 mL
8 fluid ounces (1 cup) = 250 mL
12 fluid ounces (1 1/2 cups) = 375 mL
16 fluid ounces (2 cups) = 500 mL

## WEIGHTS (mass)

1/2 ounce = 15 g
1 ounce = 30 g
3 ounces = 90 g
4 ounces = 120 g
8 ounces = 225 g
10 ounces = 285 g
12 ounces = 360 g
16 ounces = 1 pound = 450 g

## DIMENSIONS

1/16 inch = 2 mm
1/8 inch = 3 mm
1/4 inch = 6 mm
1/2 inch = 1.5 cm
3/4 inch = 2 cm
1 inch = 2.5 cm

## OVEN TEMPERATURES

250°F = 120°C
275°F = 140°C
300°F = 150°C
325°F = 160°C
350°F = 180°C
375°F = 190°C
400°F = 200°C
425°F = 220°C
450°F = 230°C

## BAKING PAN SIZES

| Utensil | Size in Inches/ Quarts | Metric Volume | Size in Centimeters |
|---|---|---|---|
| Baking or Cake Pan (square or rectangular) | 8×8×2 | 2 L | 20×20×5 |
| | 9×9×2 | 2.5 L | 23×23×5 |
| | 12×8×2 | 3 L | 30×20×5 |
| | 13×9×2 | 3.5 L | 33×23×5 |
| Loaf Pan | 8×4×3 | 1.5 L | 20×10×7 |
| | 9×5×3 | 2 L | 23×13×7 |
| Round Layer Cake Pan | 8×1 1/2 | 1.2 L | 20×4 |
| | 9×1 1/2 | 1.5 L | 23×4 |
| Pie Plate | 8×1 1/4 | 750 mL | 20×3 |
| | 9×1 1/4 | 1 L | 23×3 |
| Baking Dish or Casserole | 1 quart | 1 L | — |
| | 1 1/2 quart | 1.5 L | — |
| | 2 quart | 2 L | — |